STAR WARS

MUSIC BY JOHN WILLIAMS

— PIANO LEVEL —
LATE INTERMEDIATE/
EARLY ADVANCED

ISBN 978-1-4803-4292-7

HAL•LEONARD®
CORPORATION

7777 W. BLUEMOUND RD. P.O. BOX 13819 MILWAUKEE, WI 53213

In Australia Contact:
Hal Leonard Australia Pty. Ltd.
4 Lentara Court
Cheltenham, Victoria, 3192 Australia
Email: ausadmin@halleonard.com.au

Visit Hal Leonard Online at
www.halleonard.com

Visit Phillip at
www.phillipkeveren.com

PREFACE

John Williams' score for *Star Wars* stands as one of the greatest achievements in music written for the cinema. The themes throughout are memorable, and the rich, textured writing is compositionally superb. As a result, the score is loved by the general public for its tuneful appeal and respected by professional musicians for its superior craftsmanship. This is a remarkable feat!

In 2005, the American Film Institute selected *Star Wars* as the greatest American film score of all time. Mr. Williams is the only composer to have three scores on this prestigious list – along with *Stars Wars*, there's *Jaws* (#6) and *E.T.: The Extra-Terrestrial* (#14).

A fan first and arranger second,

BIOGRAPHY

Phillip Keveren, a multi-talented keyboard artist and composer, has composed original works in a variety of genres from piano solo to symphonic orchestra. Mr. Keveren gives frequent concerts and workshops for teachers and their students in the United States, Canada, Europe, and Asia. Mr. Keveren holds a B.M. in composition from California State University Northridge and a M.M. in composition from the University of Southern California.

CONTENTS

ACROSS THE STARS

Music by JOHN WILLIAMS
Arranged by Phillip Keveren

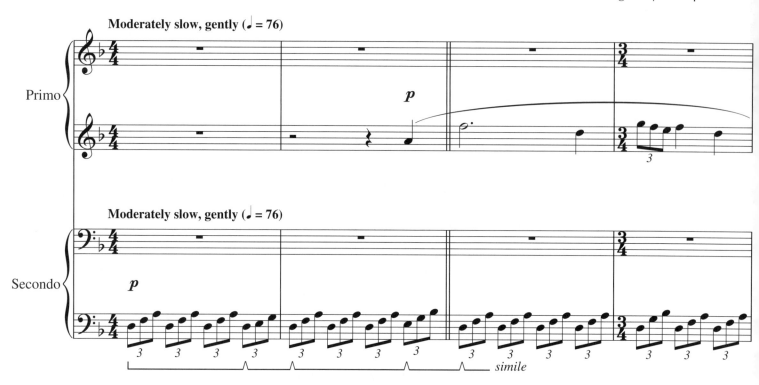

CANTINA BAND

Music by JOHN WILLIAMS
Arranged by Phillip Keveren

DUEL OF THE FATES

Music by JOHN WILLIAMS
Arranged by Phillip Keveren

20

THE IMPERIAL MARCH
(Darth Vader's Theme)

Music by JOHN WILLIAMS
Arranged by Phillip Keveren

PRINCESS LEIA'S THEME

Music by JOHN WILLIAMS
Arranged by Phillip Keveren

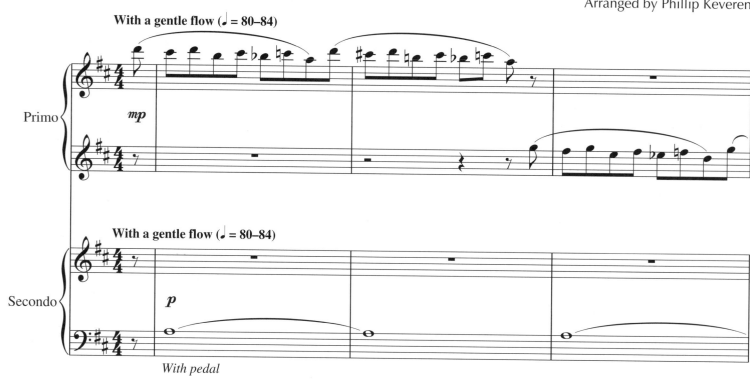

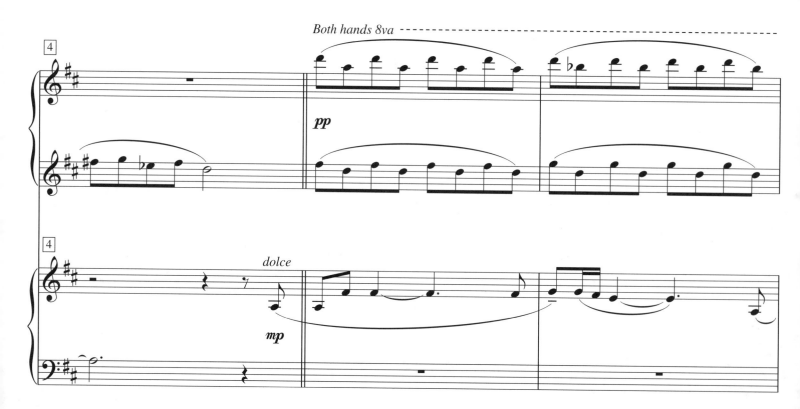

THE THRONE ROOM
(And End Title)

Music by JOHN WILLIAMS
Arranged by Phillip Keveren

YODA'S THEME

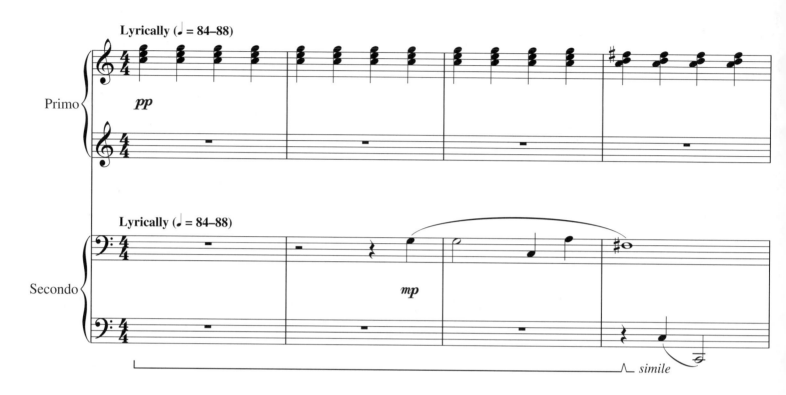

Music by JOHN WILLIAMS
Arranged by Phillip Keveren

STAR WARS
(Main Theme)

Music by JOHN WILLIAMS
Arranged by Phillip Keveren

THE PHILLIP KEVEREN SERIES

PIANO SOLO —
Late Intermediate/Early Advanced Level

ABOVE ALL
00311024.................................$11.95

AMERICANA
00311348.................................$10.95

THE BEATLES
00306412.................................$14.99

THE BEATLES FOR CLASSICAL PIANO
00312189.................................$14.99

BEST PIANO SOLOS
00312546.................................$12.99

BROADWAY'S BEST
00310669.................................$12.95

CANZONE ITALIANA
00312106.................................$12.99

A CELTIC CHRISTMAS
00310629.................................$12.99

THE CELTIC COLLECTION
00310549.................................$12.95

CHRISTMAS MEDLEYS
00311414.................................$10.95

CHRISTMAS AT THE MOVIES
00312190.................................$12.99

CHRISTMAS WORSHIP MEDLEYS
00311769.................................$12.99

CINEMA CLASSICS
00310607.................................$12.95

CLASSIC WEDDING SONGS
00311101.................................$10.95

CLASSICAL FOLK
00311292.................................$10.95

CLASSICAL JAZZ
00311083.................................$12.95

CONTEMPORARY WEDDING SONGS
00311103.................................$12.99

DISNEY SONGS FOR CLASSICAL PIANO
00311754.................................$14.99

FAVORITE WEDDING SONGS
00311881.................................$12.99

FIDDLIN' AT THE PIANO
00315974 ....$12.99

THE FILM SCORE COLLECTION
00311811.................................$12.99

THE GREAT MELODIES
00312084 ....$12.99

GREAT STANDARDS
00311157.................................$12.95

THE HYMN COLLECTION
00311071.................................$11.95

HYMN MEDLEYS
00311349.................................$10.95

HYMNS WITH A TOUCH OF JAZZ
00311249.................................$10.95

I COULD SING OF YOUR LOVE FOREVER
00310905.................................$12.95

JINGLE JAZZ
00310762.................................$12.95

LET FREEDOM RING!
00310839...................................$9.95

ANDREW LLOYD WEBBER
00313227.................................$14.95

MANCINI MAGIC
00313523 ....$12.99

MORE DISNEY SONGS FOR CLASSICAL PIANO
00312113.................................$14.99

MOTOWN HITS
00311295.................................$12.95

PIAZZOLLA TANGOS
00306870.................................$12.95

RICHARD RODGERS CLASSICS
00310755.................................$12.95

SHOUT TO THE LORD!
00310699.................................$12.95

SMOOTH JAZZ
00311158.................................$12.95

THE SOUND OF MUSIC
00119403.................................$14.99

THE SPIRITUALS COLLECTION
00311978.................................$10.99

TREASURED HYMNS FOR CLASSICAL PIANO
00312112.................................$12.99

WORSHIP WITH A TOUCH OF JAZZ
00294036.................................$12.99

YULETIDE JAZZ
00311911.................................$17.99

EASY PIANO —
Early Intermediate/Intermediate Level

AFRICAN-AMERICAN SPIRITUALS
00310610.................................$10.99

CELTIC DREAMS
00310973.................................$10.95

CHRISTMAS POPS
00311126.................................$14.99

CLASSIC POP/ROCK HITS
00311548.................................$12.95

A CLASSICAL CHRISTMAS
00310769.................................$10.95

CLASSICAL MOVIE THEMES
00310975.................................$10.99

CONTEMPORARY WORSHIP FAVORITES
00311805.................................$12.95

EARLY ROCK 'N' ROLL
00311093.................................$10.99

EASY WORSHIP MEDLEYS
00311997.................................$12.99

GEORGE GERSHWIN CLASSICS
00110374.................................$12.99

GOSPEL TREASURES
00310805.................................$11.95

THE VINCE GUARALDI COLLECTION
00306821.................................$12.95

IMMORTAL HYMNS
00310798.................................$10.95

JAZZ STANDARDS
00311294.................................$12.95

LOVE SONGS
00310744.................................$10.95

POP BALLADS
00220036.................................$12.95

POP GEMS OF THE '50s
00311406.................................$12.95

RAGTIME CLASSICS
00311293.................................$10.95

SANTA SWINGS
00312028 ....$12.99

SWEET LAND OF LIBERTY
00310840.................................$10.99

TIMELESS PRAISE
00310712.................................$12.95

TV THEMES
00311086.................................$10.95

21 GREAT CLASSICS
00310717.................................$12.99

BIG-NOTE PIANO —
Late Elementary/Early Intermediate Level

BELOVED HYMNS
00311067.................................$12.95

CHILDREN'S FAVORITE MOVIE SONGS
00310838.................................$10.95

CHRISTMAS MUSIC
00311247.................................$10.95

CONTEMPORARY HITS
00310907.................................$12.95

HOLIDAY FAVORITES
00311335.................................$12.95

HOW GREAT IS OUR GOD
00311402.................................$12.95

INTERNATIONAL FOLKSONGS
00311830.................................$12.99

JOY TO THE WORLD
00310888.................................$10.95

THE NUTCRACKER
00310908.................................$10.99

THIS IS YOUR TIME
00310956.................................$10.95

BEGINNING PIANO SOLOS —
Elementary/Late Elementary Level

AWESOME GOD
00311202.................................$10.95

CHRISTIAN CHILDREN'S FAVORITES
00310837.................................$10.95

CHRISTMAS FAVORITES
00311246.................................$10.95

CHRISTMAS TIME IS HERE
00311334.................................$12.99

CHRISTMAS TRADITIONS
00311117.................................$10.99

EASY HYMNS
00311250.................................$10.99

EVERLASTING GOD
00102710.................................$10.99

JAZZY TUNES
00311403.................................$10.95

KIDS' FAVORITES
00310822.................................$10.95

MOVIE MUSIC
00311213.................................$10.95

PIANO DUET

CLASSICAL THEME DUETS
00311350.................................$10.99

HYMN DUETS
00311544.................................$10.95

PRAISE & WORSHIP DUETS
00311203.................................$11.95

STAR WARS
00119405.................................$14.99

HAL•LEONARD®
CORPORATION

7777 W. BLUEMOUND RD. P.O. BOX 13819 MILWAUKEE, WI 53213

Visit Hal Leonard online at
www.halleonard.com

Prices, contents, and availability
subject to change without notice.

1113

mommy

mamusia

daddy

tatuś

boy

chłopiec

girl

dziewczynka

1

one

jeden

2

two

dwa

3

three

trzy

4

four

cztery

5

five

pięć

6

six

sześć

7

seven

siedem

8

eight

osiem

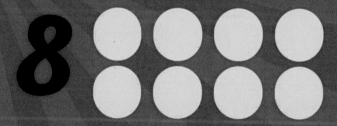

9

nine

dziewięć

10

ten

dziesięć

count

liczyć

write

pisać

draw

rysować

paint

malować

circle

koło

square

kwadrat

rectangle

prostokąt

triangle

trójkąt

star

gwiazda

black

czarny

white

biały

brown

brązowy

red

czerwony

blue

niebieski

yellow

żółty

green

zielony

purple

fioletowy

gray

szary

orange

pomarańczowy

pink

różowy

apple

jabłko

banana

banan

pineapple

ananas

watermelon

arbuz

pear

gruszka

grapes

winogrona

mango

mango

peach

brzoskwinia

strawberry

truskawka

cherry

wiśnia

orange

pomarańcza

coconut

kokos

lemon

cytryna

mushroom

grzyb

corn

kukurydza

tomato

pomidor

pumpkin

dynia

cucumber

ogórek

carrot

marchewka

potato

ziemniak

zucchini

cukinia

spinach

szpinak

cauliflower

kalafior

egg

jajko

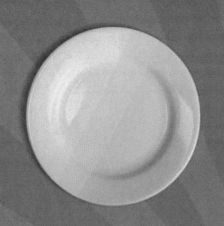

plate

talerz

spoon

łyżka

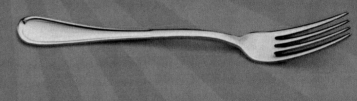

knife

nóż

fork

widelec

cake

ciasto

baby bottle

butelka dla niemowląt

candies

cukierki

cheese

ser

drink

pić

eat

jeść

hot

gorący

cold

zimny

small **big**

mały **duży**

 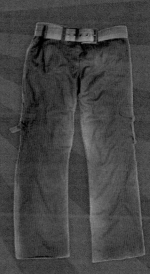

short **long**

krótki **długi**

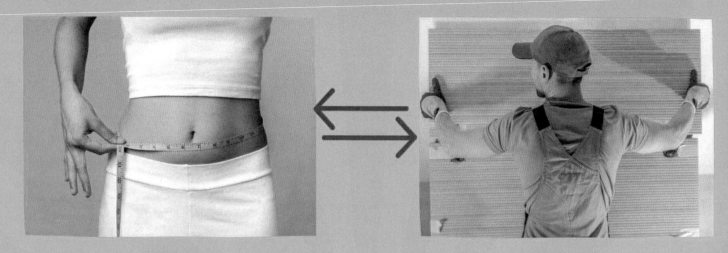

thin

cienki

large

duży

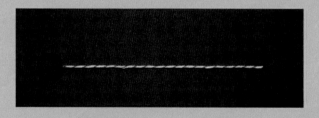

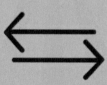

easy

łatwy

difficult

trudny

stand up

wstawać

sit down

usiąść

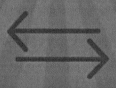

sweet

słodki

salty

słony

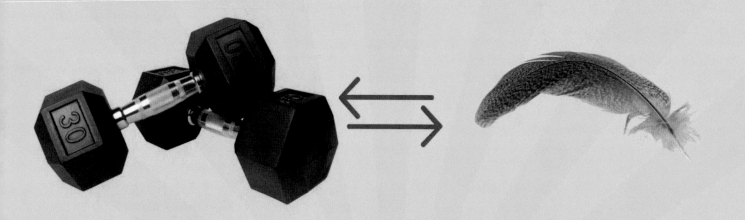

heavy

ciężki

light

lekki

in

w

out

na zewnątrz

dirty

brudny

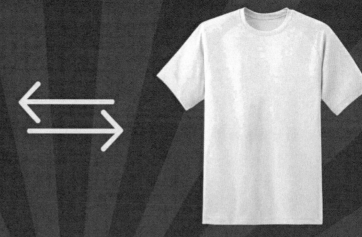

clean

czysty

close

zamknięty

open

otwarty

pencils

ołówki

clock

zegar

key

klucz

book

książka

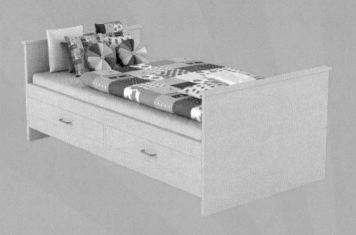

bed

łóżko

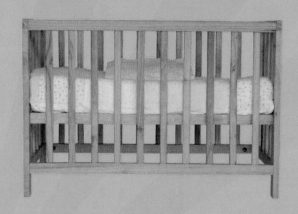

crib

łóżeczko

table

stół

chair

krzesło

car

samochód

bike

rower

plane

samolot

boat

łódź

train

pociąg

helicopter

helikopter

firetruck

wóz strażacki

firefighter

strażak

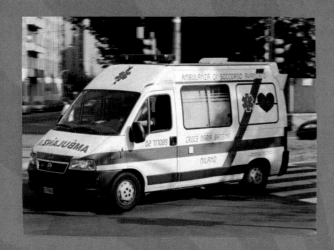

ambulance

karetka

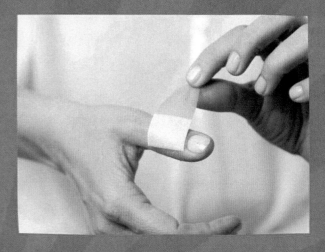

bandage

bandaż

paramedic

ratownik medyczny

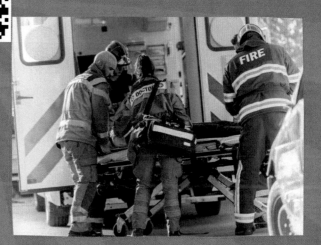

rescue team

zespół ratowniczy

forest

las

mountain

góra

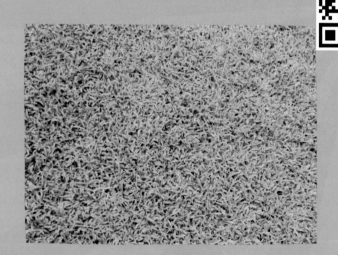

grass

trawa

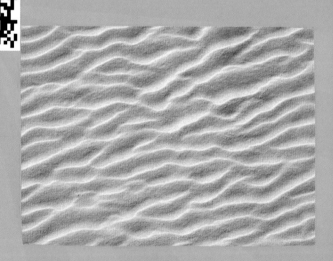

sand

piasek

tree

drzewo

flower

kwiat

butterfly

motyl

ant

mrówka

cat

kot

dog

pies

horse

koń

mouse

mysz

cow

krowa

pig

świnia

sheep

owca

duck

kaczka

goose

gęś

rabbit

królik

fish

ryba

vet

weterynarz

doctor

lekarz

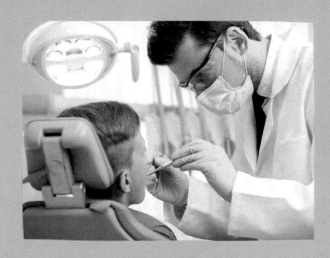

dentist

dentysta

pharmacist

farmaceuta

nurse

pielęgniarka

head

głowa

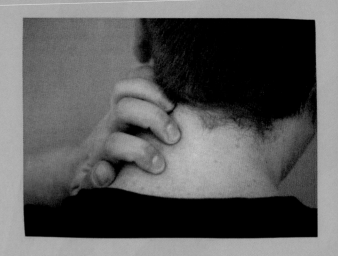

neck

szyja

foot

stopa

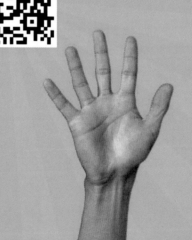

hand

ręka

teeth

zęby

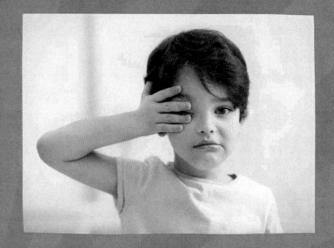

eye

oko

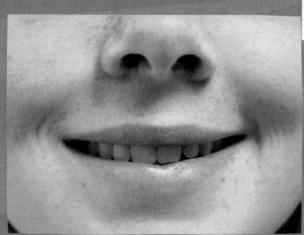

mouth

usta

ear

ucho

hat

kapelusz

dress

sukienka

pants

spodnie

shoes

buty

coat

płaszcz

scarf

szalik

umbrella

parasol

glasses

okulary

sun

słońce

cloudy

pochmurny

rainy

deszczowy

moon

księżyc